W9-CSL-243

Published by Abdo & Daughters, 6535 Cecilia Circle, Edina, Minnesota 55439.

Library bound edition distributed by Rockbottom Books, Pentagon Tower, P.O. Box 36036, Minneapolis, Minnesota 55435.

Cover & Interior Illustrations: Harry Pulver, Jr.
Edited by John Shepard.

Library of Congress Cataloging-in-Publication Data

Italia, Robert, 1955-
    Earth words/compiled by Bob Italia.
    p. cm.-- (Target earth)

Summary: Defines many of the terms related to the study of the Earth, ecology, environmental protection, and pollution.

ISBN: 1-56239-212-3

1. Environmental sciences--Dictionaries, Juvenile. [1. Environmental sciences--Dictionaries.] I Title. II Series.
GE10.I85 1993
363.7'003--dc20   93-19062
                        CIP
                        AC

Earth Words

A Pictionary of Facts, Figures, and Assorted Eco-Babble that can Help You Become a Better Earth Keeper

Use this book to improve your eco-vocabulary and your eco-knowledge. It's also great for reports, projects—or just coming up with new eco-ideas.

Use the color code to expand your search for related topics in the other Target Earth™ Earthmobile books. A color code appears on the back of each book. When you see a word in *italics* in this book, that means it is defined. When you see the Earthmobile that means there are other Target Earth books about the subject.

Target Earth Earthmobile books are divided into four major environmental subjects:

●—Water   ○—Air   ●—Land   ●—Precious Creatures

 Thanks To The Trees From Which This Recycled Paper Was First Made.

Water is a clear, colorless, odorless, and tasteless *liquid.* But it is one of our most valuable *resources.* And it is necessary for all *plant* and *animal* life.

Water makes up more than 65 percent of our bodies. People can survive only a few days without water. All living things would die without it.

Seventy-one percent of the world is *ocean.* The ocean is home to many creatures, including *dolphins, turtles,* and *whales.* We need the ocean to survive. Ocean plants give off *oxygen* that we breathe. And seafood gives us lots of important *nutrients.*

Air is the invisible mixture of *gases* surrounding the Earth. It is even more important to us than water. Humans can live only a few minutes without air. We inhale an average of 3,000 gallons of air a day. We need air for the oxygen it contains. Our lungs transfer oxygen we take in to our *blood.* Our hearts pump the oxygen-rich blood throughout our bodies to feed our *cells.* Without air, the Earth could not be our home.

Animals are any living *organisms* capable of moving about—especially *mammals.* Animals are more than just a *resource.* They are our partners in the cycle of life. They help keep *nature* in balance and they enrich our lives with their activity and beauty.

There are many kinds of animals. Those that eat plants are called *herbivores.* Those that eat other animals are called *carnivores.* Animals provide us with food and clothing. Some even offer companionship. It's hard to imagine how we could live in our world without animals.

The *land* is the *solid* ground of the Earth, our *habitat.* It is where humans and many animals live. It is where the *trees* and the *grass* grow. The land holds food and water for all living things. Without the land, we would have no home.

We need to take care of the water, the air, the animals, and the land. They make up this planet we call *Earth.* They are all connected by the delicate web of life. Lose one, and the web is broken.

Before you can take care of this Earth, you need to understand how it works. This book—and all the books of the Target Earth Earthmobile—can help you reach this goal. Then you can do your part to help the *environment.*

The abyssal zone lies immediately above the ocean floor. Animals living there are adapted to low light. intense cold. low levels of oxygen. and extreme water pressure.

A a

ABYSSAL (uh-BISS-ul) **ZONE**—The bottom zone of the *ocean*. The abyssal zone is very dark, has near-freezing *temperatures,* and high *water* pressures.

ACCELERATED (ak-CELL-er-ay-ted) **EROSION**—A rapid rate of *soil erosion* caused by human activities.

ACID—A *chemical substance* that unites with a base to form a *salt.*

ACID MINE DRAINAGE—Sulfuric *acid* produced by underground *coal* mines in areas with high levels of iron ore in the ground.

ACID PRECIPITATION (pre-sip-ih-TAY-shun) —Deposits of *acids* in *rain, snow,* mist, and *fog* (see also *acid rain*).

Over 20 million metric tons of sulfur dioxide released into the air from the stacks of power plants and other sources help form acid rain. Acid rain destroys fish populations in hundreds of lakes, steals valuable nutrients from farmlands, and stunts the growth of forests and food crops.

ACID RAIN—*Pollution* mixed with *clouds* that falls back to Earth in the form of *rain*. It is caused by the release of oxides of *sulfur* and *nitrogen* into the *atmosphere*.

ACTIVATED (AK-tih-vay-ted) **SLUDGE**—The *solid organic* waste that has been aerated and "seeded" with *bacteria* to promote rapid *bacterial decomposition*.

ACTIVE SOLAR SYSTEM—A system that gathers *energy* from the sun and stores it for heating *water* or rooms (see also *passive solar system*).

ADAPT—To adjust to new conditions or surroundings.

AERATE—To expose to circulating *air* for *purification*.

AGGREGATE (AG-grih-get)—A group of *soil particles*.

AGRICULTURE (AG-grih-cul-cher)—The work of growing *plants* and raising *animals* for food.

AGRONOMIST (uh-GRON-o-mist)—A scientist who finds better ways of planting, raising, and harvesting crops so that farmers can get more out of their *land*.

AIR—The mixture of *gases* that surrounds the Earth. For more information, see the Target Earth™ Earthmobile books *If the Sky Could Talk, For the Birds: A Book About Air, I Love Air, Intro to Your Environment,* and *Eco-Solutions: It's In Your Hands.*

AIR QUALITY SCIENTIST — Meteorologists who try to understand the Earth's *atmosphere* and how *air pollution* behaves.

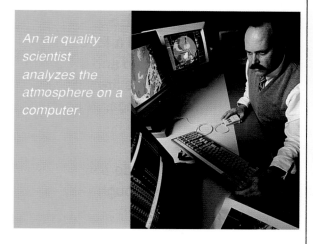

An air quality scientist analyzes the atmosphere on a computer.

ALGAE (AL-gee)—Tiny *plants* that lack *stems, roots,* and *leaves.* Usually found in *water.*

ALGAE BLOOM —A dramatic increase in *algae* growth in a *lake* or *stream.* Algae bloom is usually caused by high levels of *nutrient pollution.*

ALLUVIAL (ul-LOO-vee-ul) **SOIL**—A type of fertile *soil* that forms from *sediment* carried along by *water.*

ALUMINUM (uh-LOO-mih-num)— A light, soft, silver-white metal. Aluminum is the most common metal found in the Earth.

AMPHIBIAN (am-FIB-e-an)—One of a group of *cold-blooded animals* having a backbone and moist skin without *scales.*

The red-eyed tree frog is an amphibian.

AMMONIFICATION (uh-moe-nih-fih-CAY-shun)—The process by which *decay bacteria* convert *nitrogen compounds* (such as those found in dead *animals* and *plants*) into ammonia.

ANIMAL—Any living *organism* capable of moving about; especially a *mammal.* For more information, see the Target Earth™ Earthmobile books *If the Animals Could Talk, I Love Animals, Beastly Neighbors: A Book About Animals, Intro To Your Environment,* and *Eco-Solutions: It's in Your Hands.*

ANNUAL—A plant that completes its life cycle within one year.

ANNUAL RING—A circular line in the cross section of a *tree trunk* used in judging the age of a tree.

ANTARCTIC (ant-AR-tic)—At or near the South Pole; the south *polar region.*

The sunflower seas star is an aquatic animal.

AQUATIC (uh-KWAH-tic)—Living or growing in the *water.*

AQUIFER (AH-kwih-fer)—A layer of rock, *sand,* or gravel that holds *water* below the Earth's surface.

ARCTIC (AR-tic)—At or near the North Pole; the north *polar region.*

ARTERY—One of the *blood* vessels that carry blood from the heart to all parts of the body.

ARTIFICIAL (ar-tih-FISH-ul) **REEF**—A *reef* constructed of housing debris, rubble, junked automobiles, tires, and other man-made refuse. Artificial reefs are usually placed in shallow *water* near a coast. They increase the number of *breeding* sites and hiding places for *fish.*

ASBESTOS (as-BESS-tohs)—A kind of *mineral* (called a fibrous silicate) that is resistant to *acid* and fire. It is used in such things as firefighting equipment, brake linings, and insulation.

ASH—A kind of shade *tree* that has silver-gray *bark* and tough *wood.*

The mountain ash tree.

ATMOSPHERE (AT-moe-sfear)—
The *air* that surrounds the Earth. It is composed mainly of *nitrogen* (78.09%), *oxygen* (20.95%), argon (0.93%), *carbon dioxide* (0.03%), and minute traces of neon, helium, methane, krypton, *hydrogen,* xenon, and *ozone.*

ATOLL—A *coral island* or group of islands forming a ring around a shallow *lagoon.*

An atoll in the Great Barrier Reef.

ATOM—The smallest particle of any *substance.*

AVALANCHE (AV-uh-lanch)—A large mass of *snow* that suddenly slides down a *mountain.*

B b

BACTERIA (back-TEAR-e-uh)—
Tiny one-celled *organisms* that can only be seen through a powerful *microscope* (see also *nitrate bacteria*).

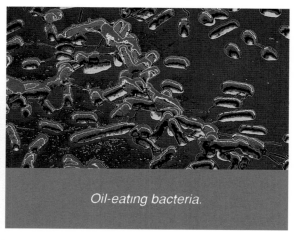

Oil-eating bacteria.

BADLANDS—A region marked by erosional sculpting, limited *vegetation,* and strangely-formed hills.

The Bisti Badlands in New Mexico.

7

BARCHANS—Isolated and crescent-shaped dunes that slowly migrate downwind.

BARK—The tough outside covering of the *trunk* and *branches* of a *tree.*

BARREN—Not able to produce anything.

BARRIER ISLAND—A narrow *island* that forms parts of an island chain off the Atlantic and Gulf Coasts.

BASALT (BAY-salt)—A hard, dark-colored rock of *volcanic* origin.

BASIN—All land drained by a *river* and *streams* that flow into the river.

BAT—A flying *mammal* with a body like that of a mouse and wings covered by thin skin. Bats usually fly at night.

BAUXITE (BAWKS-ite)—The main *mineral* of *aluminum.*

BEACH—An almost flat shore of *sand* or pebbles along the edge of a *sea, lake,* or big *river.*

BEDROCK—The solid rock under the *soil* and under looser rocks.

BEECH—A *tree* with smooth, gray bark and glossy *leaves.* It bears a sweet nut which is good to eat.

BIENNIAL— A *plant* that completes its life cycle in more than one but less than two years.

BIOCHEMISTRY (bye-o-KEM-iss-tree)—*Chemistry* that deals with the *chemical compounds* and processes occuring in *organisms.*

BIOCONTROL—Ways of controlling *pests* using natural enemies or other natural means rather than man-made *chemicals.*

The vampire bat.

BIODEGRADABLE (bye-oh-dee-GRAY-duh-bull)—Capable of being broken down by wind, *rain,* sun or by other natural processes and returning to the Earth.

BIOMASS—The dry weight of an *organism, population,* or *community.*

BIOME (BYE-ohm)—Major regions of Earth that support living *organisms* (for example, *savannas* and forests).

BIOSPHERE (BYE-oh-sfear)—The part of Earth that supports life. Includes the *atmosphere, lithosphere,* and *hydrosphere.*

BIRCH—A *tree* having hard *wood,* often used in making furniture. Its smooth *bark* may be peeled off in thin layers.

The bluebird.

BIRD—One of a group of *warm-blooded animals* that have a backbone, feathers, two legs, and wings.

All living organisms on Earth— including fish. polar bears, and penguins— can be found in the biosphere.

BIRTHRATE—The number of births per 1,000 people or *animals* per year.

BLACK LUNG DISEASE—A disease that afflicts *coal* miners caused by breathing in coal dust.

BLOOD—The red *liquid* in the *veins* and *arteries* that carries *oxygen* and digested food to all parts of the body and carries away waste materials.

BLOWHOLE—A hole for breathing, in the top of the head of *whales, porpoises,* and *dolphins.*

A gray whale uses its blowhole to breathe.

BOG—Soft, wet, spongy ground; *marsh; swamp* (see also *wetland*).

BOTANY—The study of *plant* life.

BRANCH—A part of a *tree* growing out from the *trunk.*

BREEDER REACTOR—A nuclear reactor that uses a small amount of *uranium* -235 to release *energy* from uranium-238. A breeder reactor produces *plutonium* as a waste product.

BREEDING—Producing offspring.

BREEDING POTENTIAL—The ability of an *organism* to reproduce.

The giraffe is a browser.

BROWSING—The activity of *herbivores* nibbling on *leaves* or *branches* of *shrubs* and *trees.*

BULB—An underground *organ* with a short *stem* that bears leafy *scales* or layers of *tissue.*

BUSH—A woody *plant* smaller than a *tree,* often with many separate *branches* starting from or near the ground.

The Mossback Butte in Utah.

BUTTE (BEWT)—A steep hill that has a flat top and stands alone.

BY-PRODUCT—A product that comes from the making of something else.

C c

CANCER—A *disease* in which body *cells* grow and spread rapidly.

CANYON—A narrow valley with high, steep sides, usually with a *stream* at the bottom.

CARBON—A very common *chemical element* that is in all living things.

CARBON DIOXIDE (die-OX-ide)—A colorless, odorless *gas* made up of *carbon* and *oxygen.*

CARBON MONOXIDE (mon-OX-ide)—A colorless, odorless poisonous *gas* formed by burning *fossil fuels.*

CARCINOGEN (car-SIN-o-jen)—A *cancer*-causing *chemical.*

CARNIVORE (CAR-nih-vor)—An *animal* that eats the flesh of another animal.

The ocelot is a carnivore.

CATALYTIC (cat-uh-LIT-ic) **CONVERTER**—A device attached to an automobile's exhaust system. It oxidizes *hydrocarbons* to form *carbon dioxide* and *water* and converts *carbon monoxide* to carbon dioxide.

CAVE—A hollow space in the earth, especially one with an opening in the side of a *hill* or *mountain*.

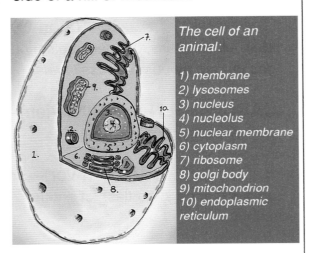

The cell of an animal:

1) membrane
2) lysosomes
3) nucleus
4) nucleolus
5) nuclear membrane
6) cytoplasm
7) ribosome
8) golgi body
9) mitochondrion
10) endoplasmic reticulum

CELL—The extremely small unit of living matter of which all living things are made.

CHANNEL—The deeper part of a waterway.

CHANNELIZATION (chan-el-ih-ZAY-shun)—Converting a natural *stream* into a ditch to control *floods*. The practice is often harmful to the *environment*.

CHEMICAL ELEMENT—see *element*.

CHEMISTRY—The *science* which deals with the different kinds of simple matter called *chemical elements*.

CHILDREN'S ALLIANCE FOR PROTECTION OF THE ENVIRONMENT (CAPE)—A children's *environmental* organization in Texas that publishes a newsletter to show kids how their lives affect the Earth (see the Earthmobile book *Earth Kids* for more information).

CHILDREN'S RAINFOREST—A children's *environmental* organization in Maine that works to protect *rainforests* (see the Earthmobile book *Earth Kids* for more information).

CHILDREN FOR OLD GROWTH—A children's *environmental* organization in California that works to save ancient forests (see the Earthmobile book *Earth Kids* for more information).

CHLORINATED (KLOR-ih-nay-ted) **HYDROCARBONS** (HI-dro-car-bunz)—A group of long-lasting, *nondegradable pesticides* such as *DDT* that are harmful to *animals* and humans.

CHLOROFLUOROCARBONS (klor-o-FLOOR-o-car-bunz) or **CFCs**—A group of *chemical compounds* that contain the *elements* carbon, chlorine, fluorine, and sometimes *hydrogen.* They are used to make *plastics* and other solutions.

CHLORORGANICS (klor-or-GAN-iks)—Toxic *organic compounds* formed in water treated with chlorine.

CHOLERA (KOLL-er-uh)—A painful waterborne disease that causes cramps, vomiting, diarrhea, and possibly death.

CHROMOSOME (KROW-muh-zome)—One of the many rod-shaped objects in the nucleus of a *cell* that become visible when the cell divides. Chromosomes pass from a living thing to its offspring, and they control the characteristics of each living thing.

CLEAR CUTTING—Harvesting timber by cutting all *trees* in a given forest area (see also *selective cutting*).

CLIFF—A very steep slope of rock or clay.

Clearcut logging.

CLIMATE—The type of *weather* at a particular site averaged over a period of time.

CLOUD—A white, gray or almost black mass in the sky, made up of tiny *water* drops or *ice crystals.*

CLOSE-CYCLE COOLING SYSTEM—A way to cool power plants by recirculating cooling *water* instead of discharging it into a *stream, river,* or *lake* and causing *thermal pollution* .

A strip mine. The black layer is coal.

COAL—A black *mineral* that is mostly *carbon. Coal* is formed from partially *decayed vegetable* matter under great pressure in the Earth.

COAL GASIFICATION (gas-ih-fih-KAY-shun)— To produce *gas* from *coal.*

COAL LIQUIFICATION (lih-kwih-fih-KAY-shun)— To produce *oil* from *coal.*

COLD-BLOODED—Having *blood* that is about the same *temperature* as the *air* or *water* around the *animal. Snakes* are cold-blooded; dogs are *warm-blooded.*

The rattlesnake is a cold-blooded reptile.

COLONIZATION (KOLL-on-ih-ZAY-shun)—The invasion of a new *habitat* by *plants* and *animals.*

COMPOST—The controlled biological degradation of *organic* material. Compost can be used as a *soil fertilizer.*

White fir trees are conifers.

CONIFER—A cone-bearing *tree* such as a pine or fir (see also *evergreen*).

CONSERVE—To protect and use wisely *forests, rivers, minerals* and other *natural resources*.

CONTAMINATE—To make dirty or pollute.

CONTINENTAL DRIFT—See *plate techtonics.*

CONTINENTAL SHELF—A shelf-like extension of a continent into the shallow part of the *ocean*.

COMMUNITY—The total number of *organisms* living in a given area.

COMPOUND—A combination of two or more *elements* .

The continental shelf (arrow) gradually slopes away from the coast until it meets the steep continental slope.

CONTOUR FARMING—Plowing, cultivating, and harvesting crops along the contour of the *land* instead of up and down a slope. Contour farming prevents *soil erosion* .

Contour farming of corn and wheat.

COOLING TOWER—A tower used by power plants and factories to reduce *thermal pollution*. *Water* from a cooling tower is released into a *lake, stream,* or *river.*

CORAL REEF—A sub-marine formation of limestone largely composed of the skeletons of *coral animals* (see also *Great Barrier Reef*).

CORE—The central or innermost part of the Earth.

CORRODE—To slowly dissolve or wear away, especially by *chemical* reaction.

The shallow reefs of Ulong Channel. Palau.

CREVASSE (kreh-VAHS)—A deep crack or split in the *ice* of a *glacier,* or in the ground.

Crevasses in a glacier.

CROWN FIRE—A forest fire that burns entire *trees,* including the tops (crowns). A crown fire is the most destructive type of forest fire.

CRUST—The outer part of a planet, moon, or asteroid composed mostly of crystalline rocks.

CRUSTACEAN (kruss-TAY-shun)—Any group of *animals* with hard shells that mostly live in *water.* Crabs, lobsters, and shrimp are crustaceans.

CRYSTAL—A clear, transparent *mineral* that looks like *ice.* It is a kind of *quartz.*

CULTIVATION—To prepare and use *soil* for growing crops.

D d

DDT—An insecticide once widely used in the U.S. which was found to be poisonous to humans, *birds, fish,* and *wildlife*.

DEATH RATE—The number of deaths per 1,000 people or *animals* in a *population.*

DECAY/DECOMPOSE—To rot and return to the *soil.*

DECIDUOUS (dih-SIJ-u-us)—Type of *plant* that sheds its *leaves* annually.

A deciduous forest.

DEFORESTATION (dee-for-ess-TAY-shun)—Cutting down forests or *trees* for fuel, timber, farming, or settlement.

DELTA—A deposit of earth and *sand* that collects at the mouth of some *rivers* and is usually three-sided.

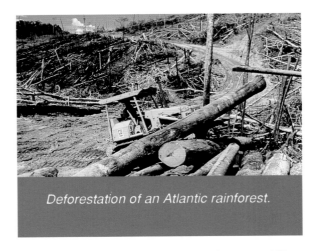

Deforestation of an Atlantic rainforest.

The Mackenzie Delta. Northwest Territory. Canada.

DEPLETION TIME—The time it takes for 80 percent of a *mineral* supply to be used up.

DESALINIZATION (dee-sol-ih-nih-ZAY-shun)—To remove *salt* from seawater so it can be used by people, crops, and *animals.*

DESERT—A region without *water* and *trees.* It is usually sandy.

DESERTIFICATION (deh-zer-tiff-ih-KAY-shun)—A process in which an area of *land* becomes desert through *climate* change, overgrazing or overfarming.

DETRITIVORE (deh-TRIH-tih-vor)—An *animal* that feeds on the dead remains of other *organisms* .

DILUTE—To make thin or weaker by adding a *liquid.*

Death Valley in California is a desert.

Dinosaurs are extinct reptiles that dominated life on land during the Mesozoic era. Tyrannosaurus Rex (1) lived in the Late Cretaceous period. Stegosaurus (2) lived in the Jurassic period. Pterosaurs (3) lived in the Jurassic and Cretaceous periods.

DINOSAUR—One group of extinct *reptiles* that lived many millions of years ago.

DIOXIN—A *toxic* chemical found in *herbicides* that is suspected of causing human birth defects.

DISEASE—A sickness; illness.

DISPOSABLE—Something that is designed to be used once and then thrown away.

DNA (DeoxyriboNucleic Acid)—Any varied nucleic *acids* that are localized in *cell* nuclei, are the *molecular* basis of *heredity* in many *organisms,* and are constructed of a *double helix* (see also *RNA*).

DOLPHIN—A sea *mammal* much like a small *whale.* It has a snout like a beak, a *blowhole,* and is intelligent.

DOLPHIN-SAFE—Tuna that was caught without needlessly harming *dolphins.*

A bottle-nosed dolphin.

DOMESTICATE (doe-MESS-tih-KATE)—To tame.

DOUBLE HELIX (HEE-licks)—The structural arrangement of *DNA*.

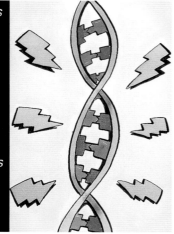

The double helix is a ladder of DNA that forms a long molecular coil in chromosomes. The chemical structure in this ladder encodes genetic instructions in cells of every living organism.

DROUGHT—A long period of time when there is very little or no *rain*.

DUST DOME—A layer of dust particles often found over cities.

DUST STORM—A dust-laden whirlwind that moves across an arid region and is usually associated with hot dry *air*.

DYSENTERY (DISS-en-tear-e)—A waterborne *disease* that causes severe diarrhea.

E e

EARTH—The planet we live on; the soil.

EARTHQUAKE—A shaking or sliding of the ground, caused by the sudden movement of rock far beneath the Earth's surface.

ECOLOGICAL ISLAND— A *habitat* cut off from the surrounding area by natural features like *lakes*, farms, cities, roads, etc.

ECOLOGIST—A person who specializes in *ecology*. For more information, see the Target Earth™ Earthmobile books *Earth Keepers* and *Eco-Careers*.

ECOLOGY—The study of relationships between *organisms* and their *environments*. For more information, see the Target Earth™ Earthmobile books *Intro To Your Environment* and *Eco-Solutions: It's In Your Hands*.

ECOSPHERE (E-koe-sfear)—The total area in which *organisms* live.

A farmer and sons flee from a dust storm in Oklahoma.

A community of organisms operates in an environment. This environment is composed of both living and nonliving parts. The community of organisms can cause changes in the environment. The environment may have effects on the community. The environment with which the community interacts is called the ecological system or ecosystem.

ECOSYSTEM—The interaction of *plants, animals,* and other natural *elements* in an interrelated system.

ELECTROMAGNETIC SPECTRUM—The range of *energy* given off by the sun. Low-energy *radio waves* are at the low end; high-energy *gamma rays* are at the high end. Visible light falls in the middle of the electromagnetic spectrum.

ELEMENT—A basic, singular substance that, combined with another *element,* forms a *compound.* For example, the elements *hydrogen* and *oxygen* combine to form the compound *water.*

EMISSIONS—Substances discharged into the *air* (as by a car's engine).

EMPHYSEMA (em-fuh-ZEE-muh)—A condition in which the lungs lose their elasticity and have trouble exhaling *carbon dioxide.*

Automobile emission.

The manatee is an endangered animal.

ENDANGERED—In danger of becoming *extinct.*

ENERGY—The ability to do work. Energy comes in many forms, such as light, heat, and *chemical,* and can change forms.

ENVIRONMENT—The surroundings in which a person, *plant,* or *animal* lives. For more information, see the Target Earth™ Earthmobile books *Intro To Your Environment* and *Eco-Solutions: It's In Your Hands.*

ENVIRONMENTAL LAWYER—A person who studies and practices environmental law. For more information, see the Target Earth™ Earthmobile book *Eco-Careers.*

ENVIRONMENTAL SCIENCE—The study of inter-relationships between *organisms* and their *environment,* with a major focus on humans.

ENZYME (EN-zime)—Any of numerous complex *proteins* that are produced by living *cells.*

EQUATOR—An imaginary circle around the middle of the Earth, halfway between the North Pole and the South Pole. The equator divides the Earth into the Northern Hemisphere and the Southern Hemisphere.

EROSION—The gradual wearing away of *soil* or rock by *wind*, *water* or other geological forces (see also *accelerated erosion*).

Wind and water cause erosion of rocks.

ESTUARY (ESS-tew-air-e)— An arm or *inlet* of the *sea* that extends inland to meet the mouth of a *river.*

ETHANOL—An alcohol-based fuel made by fermenting sugars and starches (see also *fuel crops*).

EVAPORATE—To change from a *liquid* or *solid* into a *gas*.

EVERGREEN—*Trees* with *leaves* all year round (see also *conifer*).

White pine are evergreen trees.

The Exxon Valdez (bottom ship) spills oil into Prince William Sound.

EXPERIMENT—A step in the scientific method in which *hypotheses* are tested (see also *observation*).

EXOTIC SPECIES—*Plants* or *animals* that are introduced to an *ecosystem* from distant places and create a new set of problems.

EXPLOITATION—The overuse, misuse, waste, and destruction of *natural resources*.

EXTENDED ECONOMIC ZONE (EEZ)—The 200-mile zone extending from the coastline over which a nation has control of fishing and mining.

EXXON VALDEZ—An *oil* tanker that ran aground in Alaska and caused one of the world's worst oil spills.

EXTINCT—When a *species* of living things has died out and has completely disappeared from the Earth.

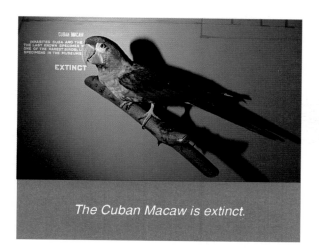

The Cuban Macaw is extinct.

EVOLUTION—The theory that all living things developed from a few simple life forms.

F f

FAULT—A break in the Earth's crust, with the mass of rock one one side of the break pushed up, down, or sideways.

FERAL—A tame *animal*, such as a dog or a cat, that escapes or is abandoned and lives the life of a wild animal.

FERN—A kind of *plant* that has *roots*, *stems*, and feathery *leaves*, but no *flowers* or *seeds*.

A fiord in Norway.

FERTILIZER—A substance that is added to *soil* to make it better for growing crops.

FIORD (fee-ORD)—A long, narrow bay bordered by steep cliffs.

FISH—One of a group of *cold-blooded animals* with a long backbone that live in *water* and have gills instead of lungs.

When rocks can no longer bend under pressure. they crack and a fault is formed. If the rocks are pulled apart. a normal fault (right) is formed. Faults may extend a few centimeters or hundreds of miles.

A flood on the Housatonic River in Connecticut.

FLOOD—A great flow of *water* over what is usually dry *land.*

FLOOD PLAIN—Low-lying *land* along streams and rivers that has been deposited by floods.

FLOWER—A blossom; a part of a plant or tree that produces a seed.

Wild flowers in a meadow.

FLUOROCARBONS—See *chlorofluorocarbons.*

FLYWAY—A major *migration* path used by waterfowl.

FOOD CHAIN—The flow of *nutrients* and *energy* among a series of *organisms* that feed on each other. For example, rabbits eat grass and foxes eat rabbits. See *The Stream Team: On Patrol* and *Intro to Your Environment.*

FOOD WEB—A connected series of *food chains.* See *The Stream Team: On Patrol* and *Intro to Your Environment.*

FORESTER—A scientist who studies trees and forests, and is responsible for making sure the forest is used in the best way possible. For more information, see the Target Earth™ Earthmobile book *Eco-Careers.*

FOSSIL FUELS—Fuels produced by the remains of prehistoric plants and *organisms.* They include oil, coal, and natural gas.

FREONS—Fluorocarbon *compounds* used in refrigerators, air conditioners, and aerosol sprays. Freons have contributed to the breakdown of the *ozone* layer in the Earth's upper *atmosphere* which threatens human health (see also *chlorofluorocarbons*).

FRIENDS OF WILD LIFE (FOWL)—A children's *environmental* organization in California that works to protect *wildlife* (see the Earthmobile book *Earth Kids* for more information).

FRUIT—A juicy or fleshy product of a *tree, bush, shrub,* or *vine,* usually sweet and good to eat. Apples, oranges, bananas, and berries are fruit.

FUEL CROPS—Crops grown to produce *ethanol* or other fuels that can replace *fossil fuels.*

FUNGICIDE—A *chemical substance* used to destroy *insects.*

FUNGUS—Any living thing that is like a *plant* but has no *leaves, flowers,* or green coloring matter, and cannot make its own food as plants do.

Tree fungus.

G g

GAMMA RAYS—A form of radiation. Gamma rays can penetrate living things and are used to make x-ray photographs.

GAS—A *substance* that is not a *liquid* or a *solid.* A gas has no shape or size of its own and can expand without limit.

GEM—A precious stone; a jewel.

The aquamarine is a gem.

GENE—Any one of many tiny parts joined together in the nucleus of a *cell* that control the characterisitcs inherited from parents.

GENETIC CODE—The *biochemical* basis of *heredity* consisting of codons in *DNA* and *RNA*.

GEOLOGIST—A person who is an expert in *geology*.

GEOLOGY—The *science* that deals with the composition and history of the Earth, the moon, and similar heavenly bodies.

GEOTHERMAL (jee-oh-THIR-mull) **ENERGY**—Heat produced by the Earth from magma and *radioactive decay*. Geothermal energy can be used to heat buildings and produce electricity.

GERM—A simple living thing, too small to be seen without a *microscope*. Some germs cause *disease*.

GEYSER—A hot *spring* from which *steam* and hot *water* shoot into the *air* (see also *hot springs*).

GLACIAL LAKE—A *lake* formed by the melt waters of a *glacier*.

GLACIATE—To cover with a *glacier*.

Glacier Bay. Alaska.

GLACIER—A large mass of ice formed by snow that does not melt. A glacier moves slowly across *land* or downhill.

GLASSIFICATION—To dispose of *radioactive* waste by enclosing it in solid ceramic bricks.

GLOBAL WARMING—The warming of the Earth's surface and the lower layers of the *atmosphere*.

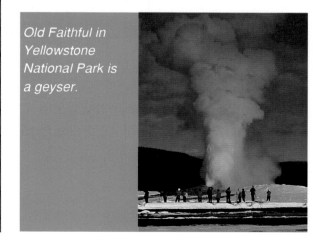

Old Faithful in Yellowstone National Park is a geyser.

GRANITE—A very hard gray or pink rock made of *crystals* and several different *minerals.*

GRASS—*Plants* with green blades that cover fields, *lawns,* and *pastures.*

GRASSLAND—An area of *grass* or grasslike *vegetation,* such as a meadow or prairie (see also *steppe*).

GRAZING—The action of a *herbivore* that feeds on *vegetation* close to the ground.

Cows grazing in a valley.

GREAT BARRIER REEF—The largest *coral* formation in the world, located off the coast of Australia (see also *coral reef*).

GREEN COLLAR WORKER—Anyone who works with the *environment.*

GREENHOUSE EFFECT—The build-up of gases (mainly *carbon dioxide*) in the *atmosphere* that trap the sun's heat and warm the Earth's *climate.*

GREENPEACE—An international organization dedicated to preserving the Earth and all the life it supports (see the Earthmobile book *Eco-Groups* for more information).

GROTTO—A *cave* or cavern.

GROUNDWATER—*Water* within the earth that supplies wells and springs.

H h

HABITAT—The place where an *animal* or plant naturally lives and grows.

HAIL—Frozen drops of *rain,* usually associated with *thunderstorms.*

HARDWOOD—A *species* of *tree* (*oak, hickory, maple*) that has hard wood instead of soft wood (spruce and pine).

HAWTHORN—A *shrub* or small *tree* with many thorns and clusters of fragrant white, red, or pink *flowers* and small, red berries.

A hazardous waste site in New Jersey.

HAZARDOUS WASTE—Waste produced by homes and factories that pollutes the *air, water,* and *soil* and is dangerous to the health of people, *animals,* or the *environment.*

HEAT ISLAND—The dome of warmer *air* that surrounds a city formed from heat-generating sources such as cars, factories, and people.

HEPATITIS (hep-uh-TIE-tiss)—A liver infection characterized by yellow skin, high fever, and chocolate-colored urine.

HERBICIDE (HER-bih-side)—A chemical used to destroy or stop weed growth.

HERBIVORE (HER-bih-vor)—An *animal* that feeds on living *vegetation.*

A cow is a herbivore.

HEREDITY—The passing of physical or mental characteristics from one generation of living things to the next.

HIBERNATION (hi-ber-NAY-shun)—Spending winter in a state of reduced *metabolism* in which all body processes are reduced to a minimum.

HILL—A raised part of the Earth's surface, not as big as a *mountain.*

The Green Hills in California.

HOLLY—An *evergreen tree* or *shrub* with shiny, sharp-pointed green *leaves* And bright-red berries.

HOT SPRING—A spring with *water* above 98-degrees Fahrenheit (see also *geyser*).

HUMUS—Dark, rich *organic* material produced by *decaying plants* and *animals.*

HURRICANE—A large tropical storm with violent wind (75+ mph) and very heavy *rain.*

HYBRID—The offspring of two plants of different *species.*

HYDRA—Any of numerous small tubular freshwater hydrozoan polyps having at one end a mouth surrounded by tenacles.

HYDRAULIC (hi-DROLL-ick) **MINING**—To mine gold and silver by using a powerful *stream* of *water* directed against the rock containing the *minerals.* This practice is very destructive to the surrounding *environment.*

HYDROCARBON (HI-dro-car-bun)—An *organic compound* containing only *carbon* and *hydrogen* and often occurring in *petrolium, natural gas,* and *coal.*

HYDROGEN—A colorless *gas* that burns easily. Hydrogen is a *chemical element* that weighs less than any other known *substance.*

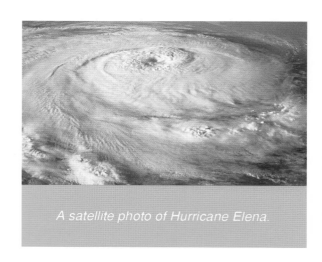

A satellite photo of Hurricane Elena.

HYDROPONICS (hi-dro-PAWN-icks)—To grow crops in a *nutrient*-rich *water* solution without *soil*.

HYDROPOWER—Power generated by the flow of *water*, usually tapped by dams.

Dams help produce hydropower.

HYDROSPHERE (HI-dro-sfear)— The global *water* mass, including water in the *atmosphere,* on the surface, and in the Earth.

HYPOTHESIS (hi-POTH-uh-sis)— A step in the scientific method. A proposed explanation of something that is observed (see also *experiment* and *observation*).

ICE—*Water* made solid by cold; frozen water.

ICE AGE—A long period of time when much of the northern part of the Earth was covered with *glaciers*.

ICEBERG —A large mass of *ice* floating in the *sea*.

Icebergs from Bering Glacier in Alaska.

ICECAP—A permanent covering of *ice* over an area.

IGNEOUS (IGG-nee-us) **ROCK**— Rock formed by the cooling and hardening of melted rock material. *Lava* and *granite* are igneous rocks.

IMPURITY—Something that is dirty or *contaminated* with other material.

INDUSTRIAL REVOLUTION—Social and economic changes brought about by the mechanized production of goods on a large scale from factories.

INFILTRATION—The percolation of *water* from *snow* or *rain* through the *soil*.

INLET—A narrow strip of *water* running from a larger body of water into the land or between *islands.*

A painted lady butterfly is an insect.

INSECT—Any group of small *animals* without backbones, with bodies divided into three parts. Insects have three pairs of legs and two wings.

INSECTICIDE—A *chemical substance* used to destroy *insects.*

INSECT LARVAE—The immature stage of an *insect.*

INVERTEBRATE (inn-VER-tuh-brit)—An *animal* without a backbone. Worms and insects are invertebrates; *fishes* and *mammals* are *vertebrates.*

IRRIGATION—To supply *land* with *water.*

ISAAK WALTON LEAGUE—An environmental organization in Virginia whose members protect America's *soil, air,* woods, *waters,* and *wildlife.*

White's Island. New Zealand.

ISLAND—A body of *land* surrounded by *water.*

J j

JELLY FISH—A *sea animal* like a lump of jelly. Most jelly fish have long, trailing tentacles that can sometimes sting.

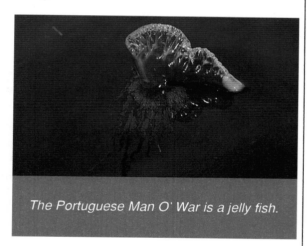

The Portuguese Man O' War is a jelly fish.

K k

KIDS AGAINST POLLUTION (KAP)—A children's *environmental* organization in New Jersey that fights *pollution* (see the Earthmobile book *Earth Kids* for more information).

KIDS FOR A CLEAN ENVIRONMENT (Kids FACE)—A children's *environmental* organization in Tennessee that work for a clean environment (see the Earthmobile book *Earth Kids* for more information).

KIDS FOR SAVING EARTH (KSE)—A worldwide *environmental* club for kids, started by Clinton Hill (see the Earthmobile books *Earth Kids* and *Eco-Groups* for more information).

KSE members outside the United Nations Building in New York City.

KIDS IN NATURE'S DEFENSE (KIND)—A children's *environmental* organization in Connecticut that works to stop *global warming* (see the Earthmobile book *Earth Kids* for more information).

KIDS SAVE THE PLANET (Kids STOP)—A children's *environmental* organization in New York that works to save the *ozone* (see the Earthmobile book *Earth Kids* for more information).

KRILL—*Crustaceans* and other small *marine organisms* that are used as food by *whales.*

L l

LAGOON—A *pond* or small *lake* connected with a larger body of *water.*

LAKE—A body of *water* surrounded by *land.* A lake is larger than a *pond* and usually contains fresh water.

A lake in Baxter State Park. Maine.

LAND—The *solid* ground of the Earth. For more information, see the Target Earth™ Earthmobile books *I Love Dirt, If the Trees Could Talk, Love Earth:*

The Beauty Makeover, Branch Out: A Book About Land, Eco-Solutions: It's In Your Hands, and Intro to Your Environment.

LANDFILL—An area built up by burying layers of *trash* between layers of dirt.

A landfill in New York City.

LANDSLIDE—A sliding down of a mass of *soil* or rock on a steep slope.

LAVA—The hot, melted rock flowing from a *volcano.*

Lava spews from Mt. Etna in Sicily. Italy.

A maple leaf.

Lightning.

LEAF—One of the thin, flat, green parts of a *tree* or other *plant* that grow on the *stem* or grow up from the *roots*.

LEUKEMIA—A *disease* that affects the parts of the body that make *white blood cells*.

LEVEE—A dike made of earth, stone, or concrete. A levee is built along a *river* to help control *flooding*.

LICHEN—A living thing that looks like *moss*. It grows in patches on rocks, *trees*, and other surfaces.

LIGHTNING—A flash of electricity in the sky; usually associated with *thunderstorms*.

LIMESTONE—A rock used for building and for making lime. Marble is a kind of limestone.

During the last 150 years. a huge system of over 3.500 levees has been constructed along the lower Mississippi River. Levees protect valuable residential. industrial and farm land from floodwaters.

LIQUID—Any *substance* that is not a *solid* or a *gas;* a substance that flows freely like *water.*

LITHOSPHERE (LITH-o-sfear)—The outer part of the Earth composed of rock.

LITTORAL (lit-TORE-ull) **ZONE**—The shallow region of a *lake* where *vegetation* grows.

LIZARD—A *reptile* somewhat like a *snake,* but with four legs and a thicker body.

The komodo dragon is a lizard.

LOAM—*Soil* composed of *sand, silt,* and clay that is good for growing crops.

LOBBY—To try to influence the vote of legislatures.

M m

MAGMA—Hot, melted rock beneath the surface of the Earth.

The mahogany tree.

MAHOGANY—A *tree* with dark, reddish-brown wood that grows in *tropical* America.

MAMMAL—A *warm-blooded animal* with a backbone. Most mammals are covered with fur or have some hair.

The bighorn sheep is a mammal.

The mantle is the layer of Earth between the crust (1) and core (4) The mantle is divided into two parts. the upper mantle (2) and the lower mantle (3). The mantle is made up of rock that is rich in magnesium and iron silicates.

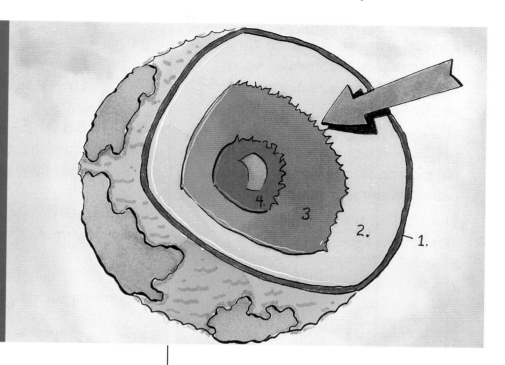

MANTLE—The layer of Earth lying between its *crust* and its *core*.

MAPLE—A *tree* with hard, light-colored *wood* and *leaves* with deep notches and winged *seeds* that grow in pairs.

The koala bear is a marsupial.

MARINE—Having to do with or living in the *sea*.

MARINE ZOOLOGY—The *science* of studying *animals* who live in the *sea* (see also *zoology*).

MARKET HUNTER—A hunter who kills large number of game for sale to the food industry. See *Eco-Solutions: It's In Your Hands*.

MARSH—An area of low-lying *wetlands*, including *swamps* and *bogs*.

MARSUPIAL (marr-SOO-pee-ull)—A *mammal* that carries its young in a pouch. Kangaroos and opossums are marsupials.

MERCURY—A silver-white poisonous metallic *element*. It is used in thermometers, barometers, vapor lamps, batteries, and *chemical pesticides.*

MESA—A high, steep hill that has a flat top and stands alone. A mesa is usually larger and steeper than a *butte.*

A mesa in New Mexico.

METABOLISM—The biological and *chemical* processes that sustain life in an *organism.*

METAMORPHIC ROCK—Rock changed by heat and pressure. *Slate* is a metamorphic rock that is formed by *shale,* a *sedimentary* rock.

METHANOL—A fuel alternative to gasoline.

MICROBE—See *microorganism.*

MICROSCOPE—An instrument with a lens or combination of lenses for making small things look larger.

MICROHABITAT—The *environment* of an individual *organism.*

MICROORGANISM—Tiny *organisms* such as *bacteria.*

MIGRATION—Seasonal movement of *birds* and *mammals.*

Snow geese during migration.

MINERAL—Any substance that is not a *plant, animal,* or another living thing.

MOLD—A wolly or furry *fungus*, often greenish in color, that appears on food and other *animal* or *vegetable substances* when they are left too long in a warm, moist place.

Mold growing on strawberries.

MOLECULE—The smallest particle into which a substance can be divided without *chemical* change.

MONSOON—A seasonal wind of the Indian Ocean and southern Asia; usually accompanied by heavy *rains*.

MORAINE—Glacier-borne debris (rocks, gravel, silt) carried by *rivers* of *ice*.

MOSS—The very soft, small, green *plants* that grow close together like a carpet on the ground, on rocks, or on *trees*.

Mt. Hood in Oregon.

MOUNTAIN—A very high hill.

MULCH—Dead *plant* material that is spread on the ground to help plants grow.

MULTIPLE USE—The idea that a given resource, like a forest, may have many uses, such as timber, *erosion* control, and *wildlife habitats*.

Moss clings to a big leaf maple tree.

N n

NATIONAL AUDUBON SOCIETY—An organization started by William Brewster that is dedicated to the protection of *birds* and the *environment* (see the Earthmobile book *Eco-Groups* for more information).

NATIONAL GEOGRAPHIC SOCIETY—An *ecology* group in Washington, DC, that publishes the *National Geographic* magazine (see the Earthmobile book *Eco-Groups* for more information).

NATURE CONSERVANCY—An organization that uses donor money to buy *land* and preserve it from development (see the Earthmobile book *Eco-Groups* for more information).

NATURAL GAS—*Gas* that comes from the Earth's *crust*.

NATURALIST—A person who studies natural history, including *botany*, *zoology*, and *ecology*.

NATURAL RESOURCES—Any part of the world of nature that has value to humans.

NATURAL SELECTION—The process by which weak *organisms* are eliminated by *predators,* parasites, and competition. The strongest survive to breed and pass on their strong traits to their offspring.

NICHE—*Habitat* and role of an *organism* in an *ecosystem*.

NIMBY (Not In My Back Yard) SYNDROME—Opposing the placement of a waste dump in one's *community*.

NITRATE BACTERIA—*Bacteria* that have the ability to *recycle nitrogen*.

NITROGEN—A *gas* that has no color or smell. Nitrogen makes up almost four-fifths of the Earth's *air*.

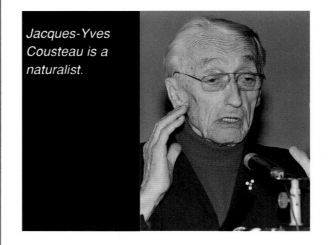

Jacques-Yves Cousteau is a naturalist.

NITROGEN OXIDES—Colorless, odorless *pollutants* created by burning *fossil fuels* which mix with *water* in the *atmosphere* to form *acid rain.*

NONBIODEGRADABLE—Not capable of being efficiently broken down by *wind, rain,* sun or other natural processes.

An oak tree.

NON-POINT SOURCE POLLUTION—*Pollution* that comes in small amounts from many different sources (see also *point source pollution*). For more infomation, see *The Stream Team: On Patrol.*

NONRENEWABLE RESOURCES—*Resources* such as *coal, oil,* and *minerals* that cannot be replaced or regenerated.

NUCLEIC ACID—Any of various *acids* (as an *RNA* or *DNA*) composed of sugar or derivative of sugar, phosphoric acid, and a base and found in *cell* nuclei.

NUTRIENT—A substance that nourishes *plants* or *animals.*

O o

OAK—A *tree* or *shrub* with hard, strong *wood* and nuts which are called acorns.

OASIS—A place in the *desert* where there is *water* and where *trees* and *plants* can grow.

An oasis in Tunisia.

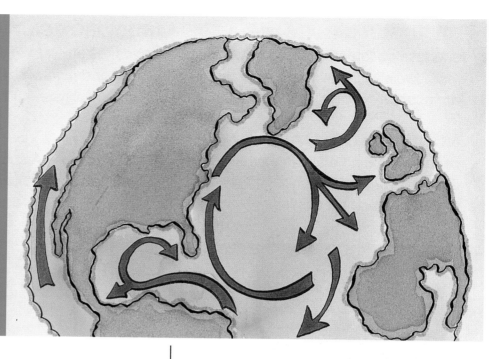

Ocean currents are broad. slow water drifts that move in a certain direction. Surface currents generally flow clockwise in the Northern Hemisphere and counterclockwise in the Southern Hemisphere. Oceans also have deep currents caused by salt and temperature variations.

OBSERVATION—The first step in the scientific method (see also *experiment* and *hypothesis*).

OCEAN—The bodies of *salt water* that cover over two-thirds of the Earth's surface. There are five major *oceans:* the Atlantic, Pacific, Indian, Arctic, and Antarctic.

OCEAN CURRENTS—Movement of *water* in the *seas.*

OCEANOGRAPHER—A scientist who studies the *oceans* and *seas,* trying to understand *marine plants* and *animals,* the way waves and currents affect coastal areas and *weather*, and the geography of the deep *ocean* bottom.

OCEANOGRAPHY—A body of *science* dealing with the *ocean.*

OIL—A dark-colored *liquid* found in the Earth; *petroleum.*

The brown bear is an omnivore.

OMNIVORE (AHM-nih-vor)—An *animal* that eats both *plant* and animal matter.

ORGAN—Any part of a *plant* or *animal* that is made up of different kinds of *tissues* organized to carry out a particular function. The heart is a body *organ*.

ORGANIC—Having to do with or coming from living things; also farming or gardening methods in which *chemicals* are not used.

ORGANIC COMPOUNDS—
Chemicals made of *carbon, hydrogen,* and *oxygen*.

ORGANISM—A living *plant* or *animal*.

OUTCROP—The part of a rock formation that appears at the surface of the ground.

OUTFALL—The mouth of a body of *water*, drain, or sewer.

A color-enhanced photo of the Earth's atmosphere. Oxygen makes up one-fifth of the air on Earth.

OXYGEN—A *gas* that has no color or smell. Oxygen makes up one-fifth of the *air* on Earth.

OZONE—A form of *oxygen* found high in the *atmosphere* and ground level. See *Eco-Solutions: It's In Your Hands.*

OZONE LAYER—The upper layer of the Earth's *atmosphere* containing *ozone gas* that blocks out the sun's harmful ultraviolet rays. See *Eco-Solutions: It's In Your Hands.*

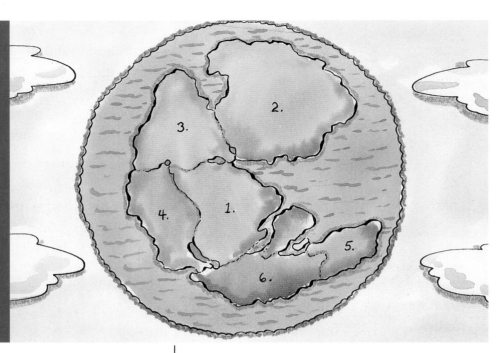

According to one hypothesis. the single supercontinent Pangaea existed 200 million years ago. Eventually. continental drift broke up Pangaea and formed the continents Africa (1). Eurasia (2). North America (3). South America (4). Australia (5) and Antarctica (6).

P p

PANGAEA (PAN-gee-uh)—The single supercontinent that existed 200 million years ago.

PARASITE—An *organism* that is totally dependent upon another organism (host) for its *energy*. Parasites feed off their hosts and usually damage them.

PASSIVE SOLAR SYSTEM—
A building designed to capture sunlight *energy* and produce heat (see also *active solar system*).

PASTURE—A grassy field or hillside.

PASTEURIZE (PASS-chur-eyes)—The process of heating milk to destroy harmful *bacteria*.

A pasture.

PEDESTAL—A large lump of rock supported only by a thin neck.

PEST—An *organism* that causes annoyance or problems for humans.

PESTICIDE—A *chemical substance* used to destroy bugs and other *pests*.

PESTICIDE-FREE—Crops that have not been sprayed with *pesticides*.

PETROLEUM—See *oil*.

PHOSPHATE—A poisonous *chemical element* containing *phosphorus* and *oxygen*.

PHOSPHORUS—A poisonous nonmetallic *element* used in safety matches, incendiary shells, *fertilizers*, glass, and steel.

PHOTOSYNTHESIS (foe-toe-SIN-thuh-sis)—A process in which *plants* get *energy* from sunlight by converting *carbon dioxide* and *water* into sugar.

PLANKTON—Tiny *plants* (*algae*) and *animals* (*crustaceans*) that live in the *water*.

PLANT—Any living thing that can make its own food from sunlight, *air,* and *water*.

Plants use photosynthesis to turn water (H_2O) and carbon dioxide (CO_2) into food by using energy absorbed from sunlight. The reactions take place almost immediately in the leaf cells.

Plate tectonics is a theory proposed in 1960 by H.H. Hess to explain the workings of continental drift. Continental "plates" of earth float on a bed of magma and push against each other at a rate of more than 2.4 inches (6 cm) per year. New mountains like the Andes in South America were formed by colliding plates.

PLASTIC—A man-made material that can be molded and shaped when heated. Plastics are made of complex *organic compounds* produced by polymerization.

Plastic toys.

PLATE TECTONICS—The slow movement of parts of the Earth's *crust.*

PLUTONIUM (plew-TOE-nee-um)—A poisonous, radio-active, silver-metallic *element* that is used as a nuclear reactor fuel and in nuclear weapons. *Radioactive* plutonium can be absorbed by bone marrow and cause *cancer.*

POINT SOURCE POLLUTION—
Pollution that comes in strong doses from a single source, like a factory discharge pipe (see also *non-point source pollution*). See *The Stream Team: On Patrol.*

POLAR REGION—The icy area of the North and South Pole.

POLLUTANTS—Man-made wastes found in the *air,* ground, and *water.*

Pollution from a paper mill in New York.

POLLUTION—The poisoning or dirtying of *air, land,* or *water* by impurities. For mor information, see the Target Earth™ Earthmobile book *Eco-Solutions: It's In Your Hands.*

POLYMER (POL-ih-mer)—Any natural or synthetic *compound* of unusually high *molecular* weight.

POLYMERIZATION (pol-ih-mer-ih-ZAY-shun)—Uniting two or more simple *molecules* to form a *polymer.*

POLYSTYRENE—A rigid, see-through *plastic.*

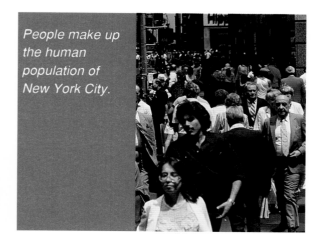

People make up the human population of New York City.

POND—A body of still *water,* smaller than *lake.*

POPULATION—A collection of individuals of the same *species.* See *Eco-Solutions: It's In Your Hands.*

PORPOISE—A *sea animal* with a blunt, rounded snout and a *blowhole.*

POSTCONSUMER—*Recycled* goods that have been used at least once and then remanufactured into new products. Postconsumer materials are better for the *environment* than *preconsumer* materials.

PRECONSUMER—Products that are not truly *recycled.* They are trimmings, leftovers, and waste that are collected by the factory and then added back into the production process. Preconsumer materials are not as good for the *environment* as *postconsumer* materials.

PREDATOR—An *animal* that feeds on *populations* of other animals (prey).

PREHISTORIC—Belonging to a time before people started recording history.

PRESERVE—To keep safe from harm.

The jaguar is a predator.

The gorilla is a primate.

PTARMIGAN (TAR-mih-gan)—A grouse-like *bird* common in the *tundra biome*.

PULP—A soft, wet mass of material. *Chemicals* and *water* are added to *wood* chips to make wood pulp.

PURIFY—To make pure or clean.

PRIMATE—One of a group of *mammals* that have very advanced brains, and hands with thumbs that can be used to hold on to things.

PROTEIN—One of the substances containing *nitrogen* which are a necessary part of the *cells* of *animals* and *plants*.

Q q

QUARTZ—A very hard kind of rock. Common quartz is colorless and transparent, but agate, flint, and many other colored stones are also quartz.

R r

RADIOACTIVITY—The process in which a substance emits radiation in the form of alpha particles, beta particles, or *gamma rays*.

RAIN—The *water* falling in drops from the *clouds*.

An Amazon rainforest in Brazil.

RAINFOREST—Forests found in rainy *climates*. *Tropical* rainforests receive 100 inches or more of *rain* per year and have more *plant* and *animal* *species* than any other kind of *ecosystem*.

RECHARGE—To restore the active materials in a battery.

RECYCLE—Reusing materials instead of disposing of them.

REFINERY—A place where crude *oil* and other substances are made pure.

RENEWABLE RESOURCES— *Resources* such as *solar energy, trees, grass,* and *fish* that replenish naturally.

REPRODUCE—To produce offspring.

The green snake is a reptile.

REPTILE—One of a group of *cold-blooded animals* that have backbones and lungs and are usually covered with *scales*. *Snakes, lizards, turtles,* alligators, and crocodiles are reptiles.

RESERVOIR (REZ-er-vor)—A place used to store *water*.

RESOURCES—The basic needs of an *organism*, including *water,* food *energy*, and *minerals*.

RESPIRATORY DISEASES— Illnesses that affect the lungs.

RHIZOME (RYE-zome)—An underground *stem* found in *grasses.*

The Ox-Bow River in the Yukon. Canada.

RIVER—A large natural *stream* of *water* that flows into a *lake, ocean,* or the like. For more information, see the Target Earth™ Earthmobile book *The Stream Team: On Patrol.*

RNA (RiboNucleic Acid)—Any of various nucleic *acids* that contain ribose and uracil as components and are associated with the control of of cellular *chemical* activities (see also *DNA* and *double helix*).

RODENT—Any of a group of smaller *animals* with large front teeth that are used for gnawing. Rats, mice, and squirrels are rodents.

RODENTICIDE (row-DEN-tih-side)—A *chemical substance* used to destroy *rodents* such as rats and mice.

ROOT—A part of a *plant* that grows down into the *soil,* to hold the plant in place, to absorb *water* and food from the soil, and often to store food.

RUNOFF WATER—The *water* that flows over the *land* surface after rainfall or snowmelt, eventually forming *streams, lakes,* and *marshes.*

RURAL—Having to do with the country.

Farms are in rural areas.

S s

SALINIZATION (sal-ih-nih-ZAY-shun)—The evaporation of salty *water* that leaves *salt* on the *land* and makes *soil* useless for crop production.

SALT—A white *substance* found in the Earth and in *sea water.*

SALT MARSHES—Coastal flat land subject to overflow by salt water (see also *marshes*).

SAND—Tiny grains of broken rock.

SANDSTONE—A kind of rock formed mostly of *sand.*

SAVANNA—A grassy plain with few or no *trees.*

A savanna in Tanzania. Africa.

SCALE—One of the thin, flat, hard plates forming the outer covering of some *fish, snakes,* and *lizards.*

SCAVENGER—An *animal* that relies on other animals to kill or collect food and feeds off the remains.

The endangered Andean condor is a scavenger.

SCIENCE—Knowledge based on observations and tested truths.

SCUBA (**S**elf-**C**ontained **U**nderwater **B**reathing **A**pparatus)— A portable breathing device used for underwater exploration. See the Target Earth™ Earthmobile book *Earth Keepers* for more information.

The seabed consists of different zones. including the continental shelf and the abyssal basins (right). The basins lie at depths of 2.5 miles (4.000m) and have many mountain ranges and hills.

SEA—Any large body of *salt* water, smaller than an *ocean.*

SEABED—The floor of the *sea* or *ocean.*

SEDIMENT—Small pieces of matter that settle at the bottom of a *liquid.*

SEDIMENTARY ROCK—Rock formed by *sediment* deposits. *Sandstone* is sedimentary rock.

SEED—A part of a *plant* from which another plant like it can grow.

SEIF DUNES—Long ridges of *sand* with bare rock between them.

SELECTIVE CUTTING—Cutting only certain *trees* in a forest (see also *clear cutting*).

SEQUOIA (seh-KWOY-uh) **TREES**—Extremely tall *evergreen* trees that live in California; some are more than 1,000 years old.

SHALE—A rock formed from hardened clay or mud in thin layers that split easily.

SHRUB—A woody plant with well-developed side *branches* and no *trunk.*

SIERRA CLUB—An organization dedicated to the establishment of forest preserves and parks, and the passing of laws to protect the *environment* (see the Earthmobile book *Eco-Groups* for more information).

SILICATE (SILL-uh-kate)—Any of the numerous metal *salts* that contain *oxygen* and *silicon.* Silicates make up the largest class of *minerals.*

SILICON—A very common *chemical element* that is always found combined with *oxygen* or other elements. *Sand* and most rocks and soils contain silicon.

SILT—Very fine particles of earth and *sand* carried by moving *water.*

SILTATION—The filling up of a *stream* or *reservoir* with *sediment.*

SLASH-AND-BURN AGRICULTURE—An often destructive process in which a patch of forest is cut and burned and crops are grown for a few years until the *soil* loses its fertility. Then the patch is deserted in favor of another patch which is cut and burn. Slash-and-burn *agriculture* is common in *tropical rainforest* regions.

Slash-and-burn agriculture near Tefe. Brazil.

SLATE—A bluish-gray rock that splits easily into thin, smooth layers.

SLEET—Half-frozen *rain. Sleet* forms when rain falls through a layer of cold *air.*

SMOG—A combination of smoke and *fog* in the *air* usually found over cities or areas where there are factories.

The Ponderosa pine is a softwood tree.

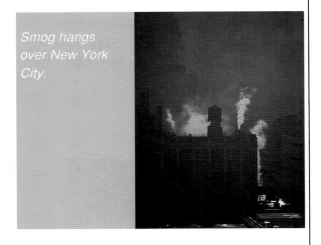

Smog hangs over New York City.

SNAIL—A small *animal* with a shell and a soft body that crawls very slowly.

SNAKE—A long, slender, crawling *reptile* with a dry, scaly skin and no legs.

SNOW—Frozen *water vapor* in soft, white flakes that fall to Earth and spread upon it as a white layer.

SOFTWOOD—A *species* of *tree* (spruce, pine, fir) that has soft *wood.*

SOIL—Particles of rock mixed with *decaying plant* and *animal* matter. Soil supports *roots* and nourishes plants.

SOLAR ENERGY—*Energy* generated by the sun.

SOLID—A *substance* that is not a *liquid* or a *gas.*

SOLID WASTE—Rubbish such as cans, bottles, and tires (see also *trash*).

SPAWN—To produce eggs.

SPECIES—A grouping of highly similar *plants* or *animals* that can reproduce themselves.

SPONGE—A *water animal* with a light, elastic skeleton having many holes in it.

SPRING—A small *stream* of *water* coming from the Earth.

STALACTITE (stuh-LACK-tite)—An icicle-shaped stone formation hanging from the roof of a *cave.*

STALAGMITE (stuh-LAG-mite)—A cone-shaped stone formation built up on the floor of a *cave.*

STAMEN—The pollen-producing part of a *flower.*

Steam rises from geysers in Yellowstone Park.

STEAM—*Water* formed of *vapor* or *gas.*

STEM—The main supporting part of a *plant* above the ground. The stem holds up the *branches;* also the part of a *flower,* a *fruit,* or a *leaf* that joins it to the plant or *tree.*

Stalactites (1) and stalagmites (2) are icicle-like formations of calcite. They are made by calcium carbonate precipitation from ground water that has seeped into limestone caves.

STEPPE—The natural *grasslands* of Europe and Asia.

STERILIZE—To free from dirt and *germs.*

STRATUM—A layer of material, especially one of several parallel layers placed one upon another.

STREAM—A flow of *water* in a *channel* or bed. For more information, see the Target Earth™ Earthmobile book *The Stream Team: On Patrol.*

Strip-mining coal in Montana.

STRIP MINING—Taking *minerals* from the surface of the Earth with giant earth-moving machines.

STYROFOAM—A flexible form of *plastic* used for packaging.

SUBSTANCE—What a thing consists of; matter; material.

SULFUR—A light-yellow *chemical element* that is used in making matches and gunpowder.

SULFUR DIOXIDE—A bad-smelling *toxic gas* formed by burning *coal.*

Cypress Swamp in Louisiana.

SWAMP—Wet, soft *land; bog; marsh* (see also *wetland*).

SYCAMORE (SICK-uh-more)—A kind of shade *tree* with large *leaves* and light-colored *bark* that peels off in tiny *scales.*

The sycamore tree.

SYMBIOSIS (sim-bee-OH-sis)—The interaction between two *species* living close together that is good for both.

SYNTHETIC—Something that does not occur in nature and is made only by people, such as *plastic*.

T t

TARGET EARTH—A study and reward program for schools, sponsored by Target Stores (see the Earthmobile book *Earth Kids* for more information).

Target Earth encourages students to care for the environment.

TEAK—A tall, East Indian timber *tree* that has yellowish brown *wood.*

TEMPERATURE—The degree of heat or cold.

THERMAL POLLUTION—An increase or decrease in *water temperature* that damages *organisms* in *lakes, rivers, streams,* and other bodies of water (see also *pollution*).

THIRD WORLD—A name often used for the world's poor nations, located primarily in the *tropics* in Asia, Central America, South America and Africa.

THREATENED SPECIES—*Species* that are likely to become *endangered* in the near future.

TIDE—The rise and fall of the *ocean* about every twelve hours, caused by the pull of the moon and the sun.

The teak tree.

TIDAL WAVE—A large, destructive *ocean* wave produced by an *earthquake* or strong *wind*.

TIMBERLINE—The upper limit of *tree* growth on *mountains* or *polar regions*.

TISSUE—A *substance* that forms the parts of living things.

TOPOGRAPHICAL (top-o-GRAF-ih-kull) MAP—A map with contour lines that shows the surface features of a place or region.

TOPSOIL—The top part of the *soil* that has most of the *nutrients* that *plants* need to grow.

A tornado has winds that range from 100 to 300 miles (160 to 483 km) per hour.

TORNADO—A very violent and destructive whirlwind, usually associated with a severe *thunderstorm*, frequent *lightning*, and *hail*.

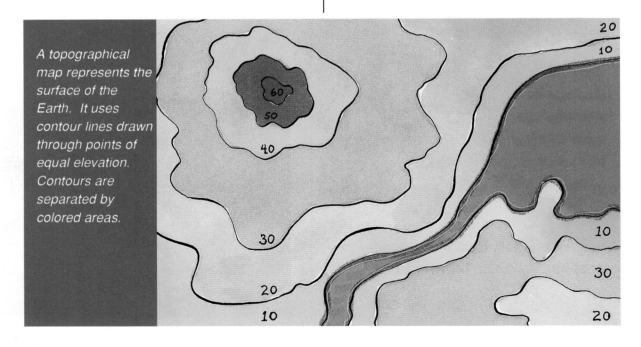

A topographical map represents the surface of the Earth. It uses contour lines drawn through points of equal elevation. Contours are separated by colored areas.

TOXIC—Of, relating to, or caused by a poison.

TOXICOLOGIST (tox-ih-KOLL-o-gist)—A scientist who finds out if people are getting sick because of a *chemical,* and where that chemical came from. For more information, see the Target Earth™ Earthmobile book *Eco-Careers.*

The frozen tundra in northern Canada.

TRASH—Objects that are thrown away (see also *solid waste*).

TREE—A large *plant* with a woody trunk and usually having *branches* and *leaves* at some distance from the ground.

TROPICAL RAINFOREST—(see *rainforest*).

TROPICS—The warmest regions of Earth near the *equator.*

TROPOSPHERE (TROW-poe-sfear)—The layer of *atmosphere* that extends from the Earth's surface to a height of about 10 miles. See *Intro to Your Environment.*

TRUNK—The main *stem* of a *tree,* from which *branches* and *roots* grow.

TUBERCULOSIS (too-ber-kew-LOW-sis)—A *disease* that usually affects the lungs.

TUNDRA—A *biome* that has less than 10 inches of *rain* per year, subzero winter *temperatures,* and low-lying *vegetation.* Can be found in northern Canada, Europe, and Asia.

TURTLE—A *reptile* with a soft, rounded body enclosed in a hard shell into which many kinds can draw their head, legs, and tail.

The Hawaiian green sea turtle.

U u

V v

UNITED EARTH—An environmental organization in New York City, founded by Claes Nobel, that promotes ethical responsibility for nature and humanity through recognition, education, and action.

URBAN—Having to do with a city or town. See the Target Earth™ Earthmobile book *Beastly Neighbors: A Book About Animals* for more information.

Houston. Texas. is an urban area.

URANIUM—A *radioactive*, metallic chemical *element* used to fuel nuclear reactors.

VAPOR—*Steam* from boiling *water; fog;* mist.

VEGETATION—*Plant* life or total plant cover.

VEIN—One of the *blood* vessels that carry blood to the heart from all parts of the body; also a crack or layer in rock filled with a different material.

VERTEBRATE—An *animal* that has a backbone. *Fishes, amphibians, reptiles, birds,* and *mammals* are vertebrates.

The wolf is a vertebrate.

W w

VINE—Any *plant* with a long, slender *stem* that grows along the ground or that climbs by attaching itself to a wall, *tree,* or other support.

VIRUS—A very tiny thing that causes a disease, and can only reproduce inside the *cells* of living things.

VOLCANO—An opening in the surface of the Earth through which *lava, gases,* and ashes are forced.

WALRUS—A large *sea animal* of the *arctic* regions, resembling a seal but having long tusks.

WARM-BLOODED—Having *blood* that stays at about the same *temperature* no matter what the temperature is of the *air* or *water* around the *animal.* Dogs are warm-blooded; *snakes* are *cold-blooded.*

WATER—The *liquid* that fills the *oceans, rivers, lakes,* and *ponds,* and falls from the sky as *rain.* For more information, see the Target Earth™ Earthmobile books *If the Waters Could Talk, I Love Water, Every Drop Counts—A Book About Water,* and *The Stream Team—On Patrol.*

Central-vent volcanoes erupt (1) molten igneous matter (lava) and (2) gases from a single pipe. A magma chamber (3) underlies many volcanoes. Pressure in the main vent (4) may open side vents (5).

The sun's heat powers the water cycle. Water (1) evaporates from seas. lakes. and rivers. condenses as clouds (2). then falls on land as precipitation (rain [3] and snow [4]). Water collects in seas. lakes. and rivers where the sun's heat begins the cycle again.

WATER CYCLE—A cycle in nature by which *water* evaporates from *oceans, lakes,* and *rivers* and returns to them as *rain* or *snow.*

WATERFALL—A fall of *water* from a high place.

Wetlands in Superior National Forest. Minnesota.

WATERSHED—The total area drained by a *stream* or *river.*

WATER TABLE—The upper level of water-saturated ground.

WEATHER—The record of *temperature,* precipitation, relative humidity, and wind velocity over a short period such as a day, month, or year.

WETLANDS—*Land* that is *flooded* part or all of the time. Wetlands include *swamps, river* bottoms, bays, *lagoons, salt marshes,* and freshwater *marshes.*

Y y

The yak.

YAK—A long-haired *animal* like an ox that lives in central Asia. For more information, see the Target Earth™ Earthmobile book *Precious Creatures: A to Z.*

YEAST—Tiny one-celled *fungi* that grow quickly in any material containing sugar.

WHALE—A very large *animal* that lives in the *sea*. Whales look like *fish* but are really *mammals* and breathe *air*.

WHITE BLOOD CELL—A colorless *cell* in the *blood* that destroys *disease germs* (see also *red blood cell*).

WILDLIFE—All *plant* and *animals* on Earth that are not *domesticated*. The term usually describes *birds* and *mammals*.

WILLOW—A kind of *tree* or *shrub* with tough, slender *branches* and narrow *leaves*.

WIND—*Air* in motion.

WOOD—The hard substance beneath the *bark* of *trees* and *shrubs*.

Z z

ZERO POPULATION GROWTH —A condition in which the growth rate of a country or region is zero.

ZOOGEOGRAPHY—*Animal* geography; the study of the geographic distribution of *animals*.

ZOOLOGY—The study of *animal* life (see also *marine zoology*).

ZOOPLANKTON—Tiny *animals* (*crustaceans*) that live in a *lake, stream,* or *ocean* and are moved by *water* currents and wave action (see also *plankton*).

TARGET EARTH™ COMMITMENT

At Target, we're committed to the environment. We show this commitment not only through our own internal efforts but also through the programs we sponsor in the communities where we do business.

Our commitment to children and the environment began when we became the Founding International Sponsor for Kids for Saving Earth, a non-profit environmental organization for kids. We helped launch the program in 1989 and supported its growth to three-quarters of a million club members in just three years.

Our commitment to children's environmental education led to the development of an environmental curriculum called Target Earth™, aimed at getting kids involved in their education and in their world.

In addition, we worked with Abdo & Daughters Publishing to develop the Target Earth™ Earthmobile, an environmental science library on wheels that can be used in libraries, or rolled from classroom to classroom.

Target believes that the children are our future and the future of our planet. Through education, *they* will save the world!

TARGET®

Minneapolis-based Target Stores is an upscale discount department store chain of 517 stores in 33 states coast-to-coast, and is the largest division of Dayton Hudson Corporation, one of the nation's leading retailers.